Out of

DARKNESS

and into His marvelous light

Out of DARKNESS *and into His marvelous light*

Author: David P. Harvey

DPH Publishing
529 Wesley Circle
Toccoa, Georgia 30577
United States of America

Copyright © 2012 by David P. Harvey

All rights reserved. No part of this publication may be reproduced, distributed, or transmitted in any form or by any means, including photocopying, recording, or other electronic or mechanical methods, without the prior written permission of the publisher, except in the case of quotations or excerpts of 750 words maximum. Quotations and excerpts are required to be accompanied by clear source references. For permission requests, write to the publisher at the address below.

First Edition, 2012

Quantity sales. Special discounts are available on quantity purchases by corporations, associations, and others. For details, contact the publisher at the address above.

Order your copy at Amazon.com.

Printed in the United States of America

ISBN-13: 978-1479276578

ISBN-10: 147927657X

Table of Contents

Introduction vii

An African Miracle 1

Irian Jaya Beckons 5

Malaysia's Darkness 9

Overwhelmed in India 11

To Russia with Love 15

Russia Revisited 19

The Russian Flight 23

Darkness in Thailand 27

Darkness in Senegal 29

Sierra Leone Darkness 33

Foday, An Unlikely Light 37

Partnership in Bringing Light 41

ISAAC, A GIFT FROM GOD 45

A Different Darkness 51

INTO HIS MARVELOUS LIGHT 59

Dedication

In loving memory of my father and mother,

Richard and Dorothy Harvey,

who faithfully served the Lord

by living and witnessing of that Light

and who God used to bring many

out of darkness from all over the world

OUT OF DARKNESS

Introduction

Africa has long been called "The Dark Continent". Currently however Africa may not be as dark as some other continents because the Light has shown brightly in Africa since the dawn of the twentieth century. Even so Africa remains one of the darkest continents. Animism, fetishism, Islam and other false beliefs still grip the majority of its population and darkness prevails over wide areas of this continent.

This small book is about the pervading darkness remaining in Africa. In addition it is about darkness in other areas of the world. God, in His grace, has allowed this writer to visit a number of foreign lands where darkness still permeates. This is the story of how the Gospel's penetrating Light has come to many of these places.

While over three decades of my life have been spent in Africa I have been privileged over the past twenty years to visit many areas of Europe and Asia. These visits have opened my eyes to the tremendous need for the continued spread of the Gospel's Light to all areas of the world.

In the early 1990's our son, Jim, secured a job with Delta Airlines. As Jim's parents, this meant my wife and I were free to fly anywhere in the world that Delta frequents at very little cost. Now that we had settled in the United States where I had begun a teaching job at Toccoa Falls College, we would be free to travel extensively for the next six years.

During this time our daughter and her family were missionaries with the Christian and Missionary Alliance (CMA) serving in Indonesia. Later they transferred to Malaysia and worked at Dalat School as dorm parents. My wife and I were able to enjoy more than one visit with our family in Indonesia and Malaysia during those six years. We also had the privilege of visiting them when they were serving in Ivory Coast and later when they evacuated to Dakar, Senegal.

Additionally during those years other avenues of ministry presented themselves to us. On three different occasions we flew to Russia necessitating stopovers in Korea, Thailand and Japan. An opportunity to minister in India also arose during that time. In all these places we found people who had come **out of darkness** and into God's marvelous light.

The reader is invited to journey with me on some of these escapades during which I learned some fascinating truths about God's Light overcoming darkness. Our adventure begins in Guinea, West

Africa, where I personally witnessed the darkness dispelled in countless ways.

David P. Harvey

CHAPTER 1

An African Miracle

An invitation came from a Kissi believer to preach the gospel for the first time in his region of the forest country in Guinea. Rather than being elated as I should have been, I was not feeling up to par that particular day and did not want to go. Reluctantly however, I told the man I would make the visit.

After gathering some Christian musicians from our local church we traveled to the village where this particular believer wanted us to minister the Word of Life. There were six of us traveling on a very bad road but, as the time approached for our arrival, I was beginning to get excited.

A meal of rice and sweet potato greens was offered and then the little horn was sounded calling people together to hear the news the "white man" had brought. Before I began to preach through an interpreter there was vibrant singing led by the group of musicians. As I had been in Kissi country less than a year I was not yet ready to preach in the native tongue. Fortunately for me, my interpreter knew French better than I.

At the close of my sermon I gave an invitation, praying to see the whole village respond to the message of hope. Sadness filled my heart, however, when only one young man responded. His name was Tamba.

Inside a grass-roofed hut as I explained again the gospel truth to Tamba, he appeared to grasp the reality of what Jesus Christ had done for him. After reading more about Jesus' life in some additional passages from the Gospels, we prayed for Tamba and left with the assurance that he understood this gift of salvation.

Once back in our village of Yende, we had no idea what would soon transpire. Upon our departure from his village, Tamba's father and uncles grilled him about what he had done. Why had he committed his life to some person named Jesus? How dare he turn his back on the fetishes and renounce the sacrifices his family had been offering for generations?

When Tamba remained faithful to Christ his family threatened to withdraw their support, including any help in finding and paying for a wife. They allowed Tamba one more day to ponder his decision. If he would not recant he would be excluded from the family and forced to leave the village!

The following day Tamba still refused to renounce his Savior so he was told to leave the family and go out on his own. At this point I was home in Yende not even praying for Tamba. When only one person responded to the gospel in Tamba's village I had been so disappointed I neglected to pray for this one young man suffering much because of his newly-found faith.

Months later, Tamba was in another market town trying to buy bread. As he approached a table where a young lady was selling peanuts he heard a song he recognized. The girl was singing a song about Jesus which he remembered from the night he had heard the music team sing in his village.

After an introductory greeting, Tamba blurted out "Are you a Jesus person?" "Yes, I am," the young lady responded and Tamba began a conversation with her that would change his life. The young girl selling peanuts was the daughter of a Kissi pastor and was of marriageable age. Tamba began to tell her his story and eventually she invited Tamba to meet her parents.

Having heard all Tamba had endured and knowing Tamba desired to marry his daughter, this Kissi pastor did the unthinkable: he gave his daughter in marriage to Tamba for a minimal dowry cost!

Subsequently, a series of events took place rather hurriedly. Tamba was baptized, taking the name

Michael, and he enrolled at the Bible Institute to train as a preacher of the Word. Reverend Michael Lai, a courageous and respected leader, eventually became the pastor of the large Kissidougou church. God brought Michael out of unbelievable darkness to be His instrument in helping hundreds of Kissi people enter His marvelous light.

Tamba and his wife were to face many trials but God showed His power in their lives by healing their daughter of a disfigured leg. This healing proved a turning point in their village leading many to believe in the power of Jesus and His authority over demonic forces. Many villagers even believed in God's willingness to hear the cry of poor and needy rice farmers. They too became members of Christ's glorious Church!

Chapter 2

Irian Jaya Beckons

After serving three decades in West Africa I found myself a professor of world missions at Toccoa Falls College. This was not a position I sought but a door opened by God and a ministry I thoroughly enjoyed for the next twenty years. During vacations times at the college my wife and I were able to embark on many memorable voyages to various countries of the world. One trip to Indonesia was a particularly impressive one.

In the introduction to this book I mentioned that my son, Jim, had landed a job at Delta Airlines where he procured fuels for the Atlanta Hartsfield-Jackson airport. His employ at Delta Airlines provided his parents extensive travel opportunities around the world. Though Delta does not fly to Irian Jaya (now called Papua, New Guinea), on one journey Delta did take us as far as Hawaii and we couldn't complain about that! From there we flew to Biak, Indonesia, landing on what had been an old U.S. military landing strip. Our trip continued from Biak to our final destination of Sentani. Atlanta to Sentani is a looooong flight!

As we flew from Sentani to a number of other places in Irian Jaya accessible only by plane, it was impossible to explain the breathtaking beauty of that mountainous land. But in that land of beauty was found such darkness. Amidst that darkness, however, we witnessed pockets of light where thousands of Irianese triblespeople had responded to the gospel.

One could not help but smile to see the modes of dress (and undress) among these primitive peoples. Having lived in West Africa for more than three decades I was somewhat used to semi-nakedness. However, gourds worn by most men in Irian were often accented when paired with shorts, the gourd protruding through the open zipper! Radiant Christians in all manner of dress shared their testimonies and we rejoiced to hear of their deliverance and salvation; to see evidence of how they had come out of darkness into God's marvelous light.

In Sentani we visited the MK school where our daughter, Judy, and her husband, JP Schultz, were in charge. How wonderful to participate in dedicating our twin granddaughters to the Lord! Traveling to Nabire (the hottest place on earth?!?!?), we visited the Bible School where John and Janine Schultz lived. There we rejoiced to see what the Light had produced in that hot, humid, coastal town.

Rugged beauty surrounded us during a visit to Enaratoli taken by my son, Jim, and me, accompanied by my son-in-law, JP. There we chatted with the Clair Black family and viewed the place where JP and his siblings were born. Truly striking was meeting men and women who had come to knowledge of the Light out of terrible darkness to shine like stars in their dark universe.

When we landed on the airstrip in Kebo many of the villagers surrounded our plane in welcome. After a trudge up the hill we were able to see JP's childhood home and some other missionary dwellings. JP's parents had taught at the Bible School in Kebo during all of JP's growing-up years so we toured that facility as well. Once we had seen the sites we returned to the airstrip to await the plane for our return to Nabire.

As we gathered with a large crowd of people waiting for the plane, the voice of Amakatuma, one of the old village men, rose above the din. This elderly man began to tell the people the history of how their village had embraced the gospel long ago. Amakatuma ended his oration by praying for us before we entered the aircraft to wing our way to another area. That moment was etched in my mind: first-hand testimony about the arrival of God's grace to this village in the mountains of Irian Jaya.

We had this same type of glorious experience in Pyramid where we visited the Jim Sunda's. There we met folks whose changed lives mirrored the light of the Gospel and whose hope of heaven was secured because they had seen and accepted the Light.

Only God knows the sacrifices, suffering, and trials endured by many of His servants so darkness could be dispelled in Irian Jaya (Papua). Whether pilots or evangelists, teachers or translators, their perseverance has paid eternal dividends as multiple thousands are now part of God's family in that land.

Chapter 3

Malaysia's Darkness

In certain areas of Malaysia the darkness can be tangibly *felt*. At least I experienced that feeling during a visit to Penang. Joining with a multitude of other tourists in a temple area filled with boutiques and open stalls selling mostly cloth goods, the heavy feeling of darkness seemed omnipresent.

In this predominately Muslim land (60%), Buddhists, Hindus, Confucians and Taoists also comprise a good part of the population. Buddhist altars can be found in many homes and shops ensuring a prevalent darkness throughout the land.

However there are bright spots of light including the Dalat School for missionary children in Penang whose influence reaches far beyond its own compound. Christian Chinese churches and other sources of light give evidence to the gospel truth on the island.

Visits to Penang, Malaysia, evoke such wonderful memories in my mind. Times of play with my grandchildren, preaching at the church at Dalat School, eating out with the family at the Stalls or Sizzlin' Chicken on the beach are just a few.

While visiting our daughter and her family who were serving at Dalat School, we were invited to speak at their staff conference held on the nearby island of Langkawi. This proved to be a picturesque island approached mainly by ferry.

What beauty! What serenity! What perfect weather to enjoy the wonders of God's creation while, at the same time, having fellowship with God's servants on this island of tranquility. Yet even amidst that serenity there was darkness. While we enjoyed sweet communion with the saints, signs of darkness and despair were pervasive as others sought only pleasure in the beauty of these secluded beaches.

It is difficult to *explain* or *describe* such darkness. When one visits a Buddhist temple in Malaysia or passes altars on the street, the heaviness is almost palpable. It seems to "penetrate" one's very being. Darkness can be felt in America too, but not to the same extent it is when visiting Southeast Asia.

Because there is so much natural beauty in Malaysia, Singapore, and other Southeast Asian nations, one could, perhaps, be blinded to the darkness there. But once one accepts Christ and the Holy Spirit resides within, it is impossible not to *feel* the darkness as it permeates all of life in some of these countries. Yet out of the prevailing darkness that is Malaysia, God is calling people into His light and glory.

Chapter 4

Overwhelmed in India

An African friend of mine spent a week visiting New York City. When he returned to Africa he told his friends "all about America." Unfortunately he based his entire conception of the United States solely on his experiences in New York City.

During a short visit to India my impression of that land may have suffered this same short-sightedness. One cannot spend mere weeks in a country and then hope to understand the land in its entirety. But I must admit, my few weeks in India gave me a "feel" that was far different than that of any other country I have ever visited.

As I traveled by train from Delhi to Dehradun and from Ludhiana to Agra, piles of garbage were highly visible along the railroad tracks outside the train windows. It was not long before I realized the presence of visible garbage was a factor in much of the North Indian countryside.

Traveling by car it was obvious that animals ruled the roads. Monkeys were prevalent and, unlike in Africa where they hurriedly scampered away from oncoming vehicles, in India they stood on the roadsides awaiting handouts! Elephants would leisurely cross highways and, in cities, cows lay in the middle of the street during rush hour. All of this animal-caused chaos would hardly be tolerated anywhere else in the world.

The darkness of that land threatened to overwhelm me. Temples provided a place for people to offer sacrifices to the gods. Other people sought forgiveness for sin by bathing in the Ganges River. To view these practices was very disturbing to an enlightened heart.

But out of all this darkness the bright, shining lights of Christian believers shone. Those whose lives had been changed were a bold witness, striving to see strongholds of darkness fall to the power of the Light. Scores of committed believers in Christ met together at a church growth conference where I was speaking. Luther New Theological College in Northwestern India was training hundreds of young people to be His witnesses throughout India.

One congregation of believers met in the city of Agra, home of the Taj Mahal. When I arrived to speak to them for the hour they had allotted, the place was packed. After the message the leader of the assembly asked me to give a blessing to those remaining. This request was new to me and I was not sure what they expected. The leader informed me that they only wanted to be "blessed according to their need."

The hundreds of people, each wanting my special blessing for their particular need, threatened to overwhelm me. After hearing each need I would ask God's blessing upon them. Two hours and a missed train back to Delhi later; I had finally heard the last story. (Thankfully, due to God's provision, I did make it back just in time for my flight to Paris!).

Each family or individual's request for blessing intrigued me. Some desired health, wealth, marriage, children, safety, power in living, purity of life, victory over temptation, or deliverance from satanic attack. Never had I prayed publically for so long and I was exhausted. Others, some having waited up to two hours, had to be exhausted as well but we felt the presence of God in that place. His light was a stark contrast to the darkness I had just witnessed during my visit to the Taj Mahal. What a wonderful way to be "spent" for Christ by sharing His Light with people in other lands!

Chapter 5

To Russia with Love

Christmas Day of 1993 found us descending toward the Moscow airport in the middle of a Russian winter. Because we carried quite a large sum of cash we were a bit nervous going through the formal procedures of customs. These funds would later be passed along to missionary staff. At that particular time the CMA was not utilizing Russian banks so the only way for missionaries to secure funds was if somebody would carry it in.

There proved to be no need for nervousness because we cleared customs and police checks in no time and were met by my brother, John, and his wife, Ruth. What a joy to find familiar faces awaiting us there! John and Ruth had been leading a missionary team in Russia for a few months already, living in Volgograd, a city some 24 hours train-ride away!

Our stay at a guest house apartment in Moscow afforded John and Ruth the opportunity to show us the sights of that city. We were very happy to oblige--at least at first. It was bitterly cold with snow and ice everywhere. By halfway through the tour my feet were freezing. Cars parked along the street could hardly be seen because snowplows had covered them during the street-cleaning process. Along the main roads only parts of cars were visible from under the snowdrifts. Some looked as if they had been there a long time!

But I am getting ahead of myself. First of all one should probably consider how large Russia is. The country is bordered by 14 different countries and while its population (approximately 142,000,000) is less than half that of the United States, its very land mass is staggering. Russia is so huge it covers more than one ninth of the earth's land area, making it the biggest county in the world by far. This country also boasts the world's most extensive resource of minerals and energy and contains one fourth of the world's fresh water.

Yet this great land is one of extreme darkness. While the Russian Orthodox Church has survived Russian communism, that ideology left behind a deep spiritual void. This country, so newly detached from communism's hold, desperately needed the light of the Gospel and this was the reason my brother and his wife found themselves there. The next decade would prove to be traumatic as, in the words of *Operation World*, "the country and its people struggled to modernize and change its socio-political structure."

After viewing the Kremlin, the underground subway system, old churches, gigantic statues, and other structures, the four of us took a 24-hour train trip to Volgograd. Having been warned that thieves might try to break into our train compartment we tried to tie the door handles together with a belt. Needless to say we passed a very fitful night on the train.

Mounds of snow and extremely cold temperatures awaited us in Volgograd as well. The hike up four flights of stairs with our luggage warmed us somewhat and we were happy to arrive at John and Ruth's cozy apartment. Showering with a not-so-modern gas heating system was a challenge. Though I won't go into further detail, suffice it to say that life in Russia during that time presented quite some difficulty!

Yet even in those conditions we found light! On Sunday morning a number of believers gathered, keeping their coats on, to attend a "prayer house" in a crowded room. While we were somewhat cold physically, the spiritual fervor of the singing and testimonies of God's grace and protection warmed our hearts.

Without even understanding the Russian language one could *feel* the passion. What joy amidst obvious poverty, uncertainty, and fear. God was truly present as darkness was dispelled in that small house of worship. Praise to the Creator and Savior was lifted in overwhelming joy and hope. My heart was gripped by these hungry Russian believers who, against all odds, held steadfastly to their hope in Christ. Out of darkness, they had seen the Light and were following Him with all their hearts. Realizing this, I decided this would not be my last visit to this vast land.

Chapter 6

Russia Revisited

When I graduated from Columbia International University (CIU) in 1994 I was the oldest doctoral recipient of that university to ever receive that honor. This was cause for celebration and my brother, Dan, planned to drive up from Florida with my mother to attend the graduation ceremonies. There was only one small hitch. Earlier in the year I had promised to return to Russia to teach at the Lampados Bible College in Krasnodar, southern Russia. Though that commitment fell at the same time as the graduation ceremonies, I felt I had to honor that promise. So my wife and I left for another trip to Russia and I graduated from CIU in absentia.

The flight from Moscow to Krasnodar was a harrowing one. Personnel of the United States Embassy had been advised not to fly on internal Russian flights because of the safety hazards. But, in our case, time was of the essence so we trusted the Lord to take care of us. After boarding the aging aircraft, we began our flight to the southern part of the country. We had been flying due south for about half an hour when we noticed the plane suddenly veer to the right. Then it veered to the left, seeming to go in all directions in just a few minutes. Later we learned that the pilots often let their friends or relatives fly the plane . . . and at no additional cost to us. How nice of them!

Upon landing safely we breathed a huge sigh of relief. Once we were shown to our apartment we realized that Krasnodar was very different from Moscow. Surface transportation in the form of comfortable trolley cars was available. And one did not even have to wait long for them to come by! The Bible College was far enough from our apartment that we took advantage of these trolley cars on our way to and from school each day.

Almost every day as we travelled by trolley car, somebody would ask us what time it was. Since we didn't speak Russian we didn't know what they were asking. When I lifted my hands in confusion they would just point to my watch. Then I would turn my wrist in their direction to show the time. Most Russians, especially those in the south of the country, did not own watches and I had forgotten that fact. Apparently my gold-plated watch sort of stuck out to the folks there. In fact, I am certain that *we* stuck out just by the way we dressed and looked. We did try to learn some basic words, now long-since forgotten, to buy certain items in the market and bread shops.

What a privilege to arrive at the Lampados school grounds and find eager students waiting to be taught. The young woman interpreting the lessons for me had almost no Russian accent when she spoke English. In fact, having probably been trained by the KGB, she spoke American English. Some of the students spoke our brand of English and even understood many of the colloquialisms we used.

The students were so excited about learning. After class, students wanted to ask questions about the material in order to understand its ramifications and how it would be used in their context. They even seemed to be more interested in how the material could help them in their real lives than they were in what grade they might receive in the class.

In addition to enjoying the company of the students, we also began to enjoy their food. Even food served at the Bible college, though meager, was very tasty in our opinion. Borsch, a Russian soup containing meat, cabbage, beets, or a combination of these, plus of course, sour cream, was a particular favorite. There seemed to be a variety of these soups, but all had that "Russian flavor" which I can still taste today!

Our memories of that time in Krasnador are precious. So much so, in fact, that I returned again the following year! The joy of seeing young people hungry for truth and light was so heartening. One cannot express on paper the satisfaction of being Christ's servants in that place at that time! For me, that experience proved to be a *kairos* moment; a moment significant at that time in Russian history.

Chapter Seven

The Russian Flight

Once more, in the summer of 1995, I agreed to return to Russia to teach at the Lampados Bible College. Peggy, my wife, was unable to leave her job at our local hospital so I made the trip alone. I really missed my wife on this trip!

The day following my arrival in Moscow I went to the airport to catch a flight to Krasnodar. When I spied the plane scheduled to take me to southern Russia I was not impressed. Not one ounce of confidence was instilled in me as I gazed at the ancient military aircraft doubting it was even capable of getting off the ground!

After boarding and strapping ourselves into rather uncomfortable seats, I noticed a bearded man in a long jacket making his way down the aisle. From a cup of water in his hand, he began to sprinkle the passengers. Likely he was some bishop of the Russian Orthodox Church, perhaps giving last rites to the "congregants" on the plane. Not very reassuring, I promise you! Even more disturbing was the knowledge that I would have to make the return trip to Moscow a few weeks hence.

Thankfully we did land safely in Krasnodar but I'll never forget my struggle to survive in that place without my wife. In Peggy's absence I did my own laundry in the bathtub. Getting my breakfasts, and other meals, in a very strange dwelling proved a challenge. But God enabled me to persevere and teaching the students lifted my heart to new heights. Again I found it to be a glorious experience, one difficult to verbally express, to teach students so starved for the Word.

On several occasions, in addition to teaching classes, I was asked to preach in villages surrounding Krasnodar. By car I traveled the back roads of the countryside with the director of the Bible School. Sometimes I preached in houses, other times in city halls. No matter what the venue, what a wonderful privilege was mine!

The Russian people were hospitable and friendly, hungry to hear the Scriptures. They desired to be fed from the Word and to fellowship with folk from outside their land. Many of our hosts would feed us or offer us large cups (actually glasses) of coffee. Though I normally do not partake of coffee, I certainly did in Russia! These portions of coffee, increased by a quantity of added milk, were enormous . . . and I never requested any of it!

Then there were the kisses! This ritual was even harder for me to handle than the coffee drinking. But for them it was the natural thing to do. Men would kiss me (on the lips!) to show their expression of love and care. Hopefully I accepted all this with gratitude, remembering the words of the Apostle Paul: "All things to all men . . . "

Actually there are many things in Russia, at least in Krasnodar, that grab ones' attention. To name a few: many women were tram (trolley) conductors; lawns were unkempt around apartments; there appeared to be many drunks along the streets; seemingly only children and young people smiled; there were a lot of mini-skirts; an ice-cream cone was only fifteen cents; people took off their shoes when entering an apartment; one always stands (or kneels) to pray; and most everyone eats soup twice a day, every day.

And there are so many other things to note: policemen stop cars for identification (and tips!); milk is purchased from small milk-wagons (one must provide their own container); cars have right-of-way over pedestrians; one must stand in line to buy bread; there are dogs and more dogs; people carry shopping bags with them (not given in stores); women sweep the sidewalks in the morning; no gas stations within the city; women dye their hair red and orange; one sees motorcycles with sidecars;

Russian people love music and many sing in harmony with beautiful voices!

In many ways the countryside of Russia reminded me of Africa: the un-paved streets, houses were not "in line", chickens and ducks walking everywhere, open markets, etc. So often I find myself wishing I could return to that place where I felt so at home. I would like to fellowship with the Christians, offer encouragement, and spread hope and light to those who still wait in darkness. May God continue to call more laborers into that harvest field!

Chapter Eight

Darkness in Thailand

An "oasis in Bangkok" is what I would call the missionary guest house in the capital city of Thailand. After the bustling streets of the city, having seen numerous Buddhist shrines and altars, we were glad to be safely ensconced in a clean, quiet, place of rest.

A pedicab, three-wheeled rickshaw, took us to the river where we boarded a small passenger boat for a trip to the center of the city. In a Buddhist temple where one could feel the darkness, the hopelessness of those who put their hope in Buddha was evident to us. Sadly, belief in Buddha has captured the minds of more than 90 percent of the people in Thailand.

Climbing the rather steep steps towards the large temple we gazed at the gigantic stone statue of Buddha. Thinking of the millions who bow to him, asking for his help for their problems, caused a shudder.

As we walked from place to place we passed a number of small altars or shrines on the street corners. Candles were lit to honor the gods, and old ladies were bowing or offering rice or other items for the benefit of Buddha and other gods.

Yet, in this city of darkness we found lights shining brightly. Missionary friends took us to a local Thai hospital where we prayed for, seeking to encourage, a very ill Thai gentleman. What a testimony of victory and grace was his! He told of how precious the Savior was to him and of how his life had been transformed since he put his trust in Jesus Christ. As we left that hospital room it was I who was encouraged.

Thailand is a land, however, shrouded in darkness. With less than one percent of the population claiming to be Christian, the religions of Buddhism and Islam hold the Thai people in their grip. The CMA boasts less than 75 organized churches (about 8,000 inclusive members) in the whole of Thailand whose population exceeds 65 million people.

Blessed with about 30 CMA missionaries who seek to bring the gospel to this needy land, it remains in desperate need of our fervent and continued prayer support! Oh that God would break through the darkness and bring light to the many who have yet to comprehend what God has done for them in Christ.

Chapter Nine

Darkness in Senegal

Some countries in West Africa have been blessed to see more light than others in this vast continent. The country of Senegal is one which has seen very little light. In the past decade however, more servants of God have found their way to that land and the Light is beginning to shine more brightly.

Senegal has a population of 11 to 13 million people, 95 percent of whom are followers of Islam. While five percent of the people claim to be Christian, more than half of these would adhere to the beliefs of the Roman Catholic Church. Though there are signs that the light of the gospel is beginning to make greater inroads into Senegal, darkness continues to permeate the country.

My daughter and her family, who were working in Senegal in 2006, invited us to visit over the Christmas holidays. During our month there we spent most of our time in the city of Dakar. JP and Judy, our daughter and son-in-law, live there and work as house parents for teenage girls who attend Dakar Academy.

Dakar Academy, or DA, as it is affectionately known, is a school (kindergarten through grade 12) for missionary children. It was founded by the United World Mission (UWM) and is presently co-owned by UWM, Assemblies of God, and World Venture. DA offers the only accredited boarding program in Africa, with approximately 250 students. All three of our granddaughters graduated from the Academy.

Without question Dakar Academy is one of the stronger lights of the gospel in the country of Senegal. Light is spread through chapel services, music and cultural programs. In addition, the outreach of the students and faculty to other areas of the country bring light and hope to a fairly large number of Senegalese.

There is much to see and do in the capital city of Dakar and in the surrounding territory. The city boasts more than 2,000,000 people with its bustling downtown, hustling vendors, nearby Pink Lake, and the infamous Gorée Island. Countless African slaves were sent to the New World from the "Door of No Return" on Gorée Island.

Tabaski, an Islamic holiday commemorating Abraham's willingness to sacrifice his son, was celebrated during our visit to Senegal. Hundreds of thousands of sheep are slaughtered in remembrance of how Isaac's life was spared by a ram. What a sight! Sheep everywhere, and the urge to shout out the truth of how Jesus had become our sacrifice for sin once and for all, was almost uncontrollable!

JP and Judy have many friends among the Senegalese. Tapha, short for Mustapha, runs a small boutique just around the corner from the dormitory. Girls from JP and Judy's dorm come in daily contact with Tapha and he knows what each of these girls' parents are doing on the continent of Africa. In spite of this daily contact with the light of Christ, Tapha has yet to accept God's precious gift of eternal life.

Other Senegalese work for Dakar Academy in a variety of capacities. Some guard the campus from intruders while others do routine maintenance on buildings and vehicles. Yacine Sagna, a local woman with three sons, works as housekeeper and cook at JP and Judy's dorm. Laundry is done in the dorm each day by Nina Coly. Several dorm parents are aided by the purchasing services of Ousmane Salle. None of these day laborers has invited the Light into their own lives even though they see Him manifested daily by staff and students of Dakar Academy.

The Christian and Missionary Alliance have sent several missionary couples to the field of Senegal during the past five years. In the days to come, may the light of the gospel find root in many hearts so the darkness of Senegal will give way to the glorious light of Jesus Christ.

Chapter Ten

Sierra Leone Darkness

Our two children, Jim and Judy, spent most of their grade school days attending the missionary children school in Kabala, Sierra Leone. It was called the Kabala Rupp Memorial School (KRMS). Kabala was a beautiful little town, tucked away in the mountains of northern Sierra Leone.

The country of Sierra Leone (meaning *lion mountains*) was a quiet land back when our children were students there in the 70s. This small country on West Africa's coast, however, has been ravaged by a civil war which began back in 1991 and continued for at least a decade. Tens of thousands of people were killed and almost 2,000,000 fled the country as refugees.

One of the reasons given for the triggering of political upheaval in the country was related to the natural resources in that land, including diamonds and gold. The true diamonds, however, are the believers in Jesus Christ, many who continue to shine brightly in these days when efforts at rebuilding a peaceful society continue to find roadblocks to its fulfillment.

Sierra Leone is a country of more than four million people, with more than 50 percent of the population following Islam, 30 percent following indigenous religions, and 20 percent of the population claiming to be Christian. It is obvious, however, that many of this 20 percent are not following the Christ of the Scriptures.

Sierra Leone, which became a colony of the British in 1808, became a settlement for freed slaves, especially the capital of Freetown, hence its name. There are huge trees, still found in the capital, to which slaves had been chained back in the years when slave-trading in West Africa was at its height. Thank God there are now thousands in the country who have found true freedom, having seen the light through the preaching of the gospel.

Our frequent trips to that land, to take or visit our children at the MK school, to visit the Wesleyan hospital at Kamakwie , or to purchase needed goods in Freetown always gave us an opportunity to see God's servants at work in spreading the light of the gospel in many ways.

The Wesleyan Hospital in Kamakwei was the primary hospital in the northwest portion of Sierra Leone. This began as Wesleyan Methodist missionaries from the United States began a medical mission there n 1919.

During the ten-year civil war, the hospital was taken over by rebels. Most of the staff was able to flee. However, one of the doctors was captured and forced by the rebels to work at the hospital. By doing this he protected his family from being killed. What a light this hospital has been over the past decades of service to the Master.

The Kabala School for missionary children was itself a bright light in that land of darkness. The Bible schools at Kabala and Joui, the MCA headquarters' station at Magburaka, the business agent at Freetown, and other places of ministry all shone brightly, giving opportunity for many to come to Christ even before the onslaught of the civil war to come.

God has his Church in Sierra Leone and those that comprise it are still proclaiming the Light. May the gospel continue to spread in that land by national believers as well as by missionaries who continue to share the Light through evangelism and teaching, medical, social, and educational ministries for His glory.

Chapter Eleven

Foday, An Unlikely Light

In the early 1900's, Sierra Leonian nationals referred to their country as the "white man's graveyard" because so many missionaries died, mostly of malaria, there in that land. When missionaries left the United States to go to Sierra Leone, many of them built plywood crates in which to ship their belongings. The wood from the crate could then be used, in the event of their death, to construct their coffins.

My wife and I often visited the Kabala region of Sierra Leone when our two children, Judy and Jim, attended the Kabala school for missionary children. Our kids received most of their elementary and middle school years of education at this institution in the interior of that beautiful country.

During one visit, I remember standing with our colleagues, Paul and Florine Ellenberger (former C&MA missionaries to Guinea), staring at some of the missionary graves in Sierra Leone. We all had some difficulty holding back tears as we pondered the ultimate sacrifice made by those desperate to bring the light to that land.

In the year 1905, the Christian and Missionary Alliance established a mission station some 40 miles from the town of Kabala in Northern Sierra Leone. During that year two C&MA missionaries died and were buried in that town near the mission station.

Seventy years later, in 1975, Gareth Wiederkehr, a houseparent at the MK School, serving with the Missionary Church Association, took a group of young teens from the school in Kabala to visit those two graves. He invited any children who felt they might be called to missionary service, to come with him on this little trek. One thirteen year-old young man, Wayne, was the son of Mr Wiederkehr. Wayne was in sixth grade at the time of this trip.

As the group gathered around the graves, Mr. Wiederkehr related to the students how the missionaries had come to Africa to spread the light of the gospel, knowing that they might never make it back to the homeland. He then asked each student if they still felt called to missionary service knowing they might have to sacrifice their very lives as these previous missionaries had done. Most of the children gathered there replied, "I will. I am ready to give my life." Mr. Wiederkehr's son, Wayne, was one of those who answered, "I will!"

Just 40 days later, on June 25, 1975, Wayne gave his life at Kamakwie hospital in Sierra Leone, dying of septic shock after having been bitten by a ground squirrel. His parents, Gareth and Treva Wiederkehr, drove back to Kabala where they held a funeral service for their son at the dormitory that very next day. Attending the funeral was an African lad who worked in the dorm kitchen. This young fellow's name was Foday.

After watching the missionaries conduct the funeral, Foday was asked by one of the single missionary women if he knew what would happen to him if he were to die that day. Foday replied that he didn't know but that he wanted to be ready the way Wayne had been in case he should die soon. On that very day of Wayne's funeral, Foday gave his heart to Jesus Christ.

This was the beginning of God's work in Foday's life. While Foday continued to work in the dorm kitchen at the MK children' school, one of the teachers taught him to read and write using the Bible as their "textbook." With his elementary knowledge of reading and writing, Foday preached his very first sermon at the age of 21. His passage was John 3:16, the only passage Foday could read at that time.

Due to the civil war in Sierra Leone the school closed in 1991. When the rebel fighting reached Kabala, Foday was forced into hiding and thus became pastor of the underground church in the region. One of Foday's sons was killed by the rebels for refusing to reveal to them where his father was hiding. During those war years God multiplied Foday's ministry and the church grew mightily under his leadership.

In June of 2011, Foday was able to make a trip to the United States, his first trip outside of Sierra Leone. At a meeting of former Sierra Leone missionaries and friends held at a campground in Ohio, Foday and Mr. Wiederkehr gave testimonies on the anniversary of Wayne's death. Foday told how, because of Wayne's ultimate sacrifice, God's light was revealed to Foday. He went on to tell of God's blessing and how the Lord enabled him to begin seven churches in the Kabala region during those intervening war-torn years.

Foday, a man with no formal education, now serves as the district superintendent for all the churches in the Kabala region. He mentors the young pastors who serve in those churches. The testimony of a young boy's life and that of others willing to share the light of the gospel with Foday have resulted in many others coming to a firsthand knowledge of the true Light.

Chapter Twelve

Partnership in Bringing Light

Out of more than five decades of missions-related ministry, none has been more fulfilling than being involved in preparing students to shed the light in other lands. It would be impossible to remember all who have participated in the missions classes at Toccoa Falls College and are now serving the Lord overseas. As I sit and write these chapters, however, many missionaries (now often referred to as *overseas workers or international workers*) come to mind. Many of these serve in the darkest corners of the world bringing light to those still in darkness. These overseas workers once sat in the corner chairs in our missions' classrooms!

Allow me to mention just a few. Some of you might recognize these names and are even assisting in their ministries by supporting them in prayer and other ways. Todd and Debbie Adams in Papua, New Guinea; Bryan and Vickie Joyce in Russsia; Steve and Cricket Volstad and Tom and Miriam Becker in Russia; Rich and Lisa Brown in Ecuador; Connie Seale in Kosovo; Mike and Ingrid Baldwin and Jeff and Deborah Climie in the Dominican Republic; Martin and Joanna Chaaya and Craig and Cathy Lewis in Spain; Trey and Tabitha Martin and Nathan and

Rachel Greenfield in Jordan; Jonathan and Fiona Snowden, Mike and Valerie Stephens, and Stan and Jaynee Walker, in Senegal.

There are many more of my previous students serving in China, Bolivia, Italy and other places, including in the United States. These whom I taught now share the light in darkened corners of the earth. And if that were not enough, this network of "light-sharers" continues to expand. Some of the above, as well as others not mentioned, already have children of their own who plan to one day serve full-time in overseas ministries.

If you, the reader, desire to affect the lives of hundreds, even thousands, of people around the world, I challenge you to pray for those already involved in cross-cultural ministries. Other than going overseas yourself, there is no greater way to support those who are there than to pray for them.

One of the most difficult and frustrating tasks of being God's servant overseas is that of language learning. Other missionaries face personal temptations not faced in their homelands. Those in leadership need wisdom and grace in dealing with issues in a foreign culture. Every-day activities become time-consuming and frustrating due to misunderstanding, stress, and complexity when dealt with in the context of a foreign culture.

Some missionaries spend so much time surviving in an unfamiliar culture that they spend very little time doing the ministry to which they have been called. Some need encouragement to spend more time with the Lord in quiet contemplation as the urgent (apparent) needs of the moment distract them.

Health and financial issues press on them. Family and schooling problems take unusual amounts of time in an overseas setting. Loneliness, insecurity, and marital problems can be exaggerated in a cross-cultural context.

The Enemy is not going to allow light to penetrate the darkness without a fight. Our weapons are prayer, meditation, fasting, and perseverance. Each one of us needs to join the battle and pray that the Light will be victorious in prevailing over the darkness in every corner of the globe!

Everyone has a role in bringing the light of gospel to those who still sit in darkness around the world. Sharing the Light . . . there can be no greater ministry!

Chapter Thirteen

ISAAC, A GIFT FROM GOD

When I was a young missionary to Guinea I often had the opportunity to visit the leader of the Kissi district who lived in Kissidougou. Paul Keita was pastor of the Kissidougou church as well as the president of the Kissi Church including the districts of Kissidougou and Guekedou.

I first met Isaac Keita, Paul's oldest child, when he was just a young boy. Isaac was an obedient child who already seemed to have his heart set on following in the footsteps of his father by serving God.

As Isaac grew into manhood, it became evident that his excellent knowledge of the French language enabled him to communicate the gospel story with clarity and power. When Isaac's father became president of the National Church and moved to Conakry, Isaac was singled out by the national church committee to obtain additional training outside the confines of the country of Guinea. The hope was that doing so would later profit the national church when Isaac returned with an even greater ability to spread the Good News in his homeland.

Isaac took advantage of the opportunity to perfect his English when the church sent him to England for six months. After those six months, Isaac then completed the master's degree program at Canadian Bible College (now Ambrose University College). The entire family moved to Canada while Isaac studied there and then they returned to their homeland of Guinea.

Upon their return to Guinea, Isaac was assigned to the Telekoro Bible Institute in Kissidougou as a professor in biblical studies. During the time Isaac and I overlapped at the Institute I quickly discovered that Isaac was not only gifted in teaching and preaching, but also was quite adept at finding solutions to various problems as they arose. Whether these problems were related to students and discipline issues or to classroom curriculum needs, Isaac appeared wise beyond his years in handling whatever issues came his way.

Evidently the people of God in Guinea also recognized the gifts God had bestowed upon Isaac. Within just a few years of Isaac becoming a professor at the Bible Institute the church constituency elected Isaac to be the president of the Guinea National Church.

Isaac's gift of evangelism was quite apparent to everyone with whom he came in contact and thus he was asked to preach in many countries of West Africa. He became a much sought-after speaker for national church conferences in Mali, Burkina Faso, Ivory Coast and other lands. Eventually Isaac spoke in just about every West African nation as well as many other countries and continents around the globe.

After a few more years had passed, Isaac was recruited to be the director of the West African seminary in Abidjan, Ivory Coast (FATEAC). There, scores of students from many African nations came to prepare themselves to be leaders of churches and denominations in their own home countries around the continent much as Isaac had been in his.

Seeing the need for even further education to better fulfill this new role, Isaac Keita attended The Evangelical Divinity School (TEDS) in Deerfield, Illinois to pursue his doctoral degree. This prestigious degree was conferred upon Isaac in May of 2011.

One month later Isaac became very ill and found it difficult to carry on the heavy responsibilities that were his at the Seminary. Not only was he still serving as director of the seminary but also as the C&MA representative for Africa to the Alliance World

Fellowship. His sickness, however, brought him to death's door and many feared for his life. People from all over the world cried out to God on Isaac's behalf.

Semi-paralysis engulfed Isaac and he lost the use of his legs. After three separate surgeries and four months of lying flat on his back, Isaac still saw no improvement in his physical condition. Despite all the trauma of his sickness, however, Isaac's trust remained firmly rooted in His God and the Lord had mercy on him. According to Dr. David Thompson, C&MA missionary physician, Isaac should never have walked again. But against all human odds God performed a miracle and Isaac began walking again. In all the darkness that had shrouded Isaac's life in the form sickness, the light of God's promises and the prayers of God's people had sustained Isaac's hope.

In addition to Isaac's struggle with semi-paralysis, his liver had been damaged and either malaria, hepatitis or both threatened his health. Another miracle touch by the Savior was needed and we know that God would bring glory to Himself however He chose to work through the life of His servant, Isaac. Sadly for those of us here on earth, God chose to reveal Himself by providing ultimate healing for Isaac Keita.

Isaac passed from this world into his Savior's loving arms and a world of eternal Light on January 25, 2012. Colleagues from the seminary in Abijan, Cote d'Ivoire immediately gathered around his wife, Rachel, to sustain her through the grieving and honoring process for her dear husband. Services were held and extremely well-attended by students, professors, and other dignitaries at the seminary in the week following Isaac's death.

From Isaac's adopted home in Abidjan, Rachel returned to their native land of Guinea, bringing Isaac's body with her. On February 11, 2012 many people from a variety of organizations, religions, and lands gathered in the Palace of the People in Guinea's capital city, Conakry, to pay their respects to a beloved friend, co-worker, and ambassador of God's Light to all with whom he came in contact.

On the following day, Isaac's body was layed to rest in yet another God-honoring ceremony in Conakry, this time limited to mostly family and only Isaac's closest friends. In the days following such grief and ceremony, Rachel, her four children and one grandchild, traveled to the interior of Guinea, into Isaac's birth region known better as the Forest Region of the Kissi people. There his people grieved the loss of their loved one and made plans for their future without Isaac.

Join this author in prayer that the true LIGHT which Isaac followed all the days of his time on earth would be glorified even through Isaac's ultimate sacrifice of his very life. May many come to know the Light as Isaac did during his time on our planet and may that Light continue to shine around the world because of Isaac's testimony and gracious love to all.

Chapter Fourteen

A Different Darkness

At times in our lives we all experience darkness in one form or another. The darkness discussed in this chapter is a very personal one. My own wife prefers not to revisit, nor even discuss, this period of darkness in our lives. Thankfully she remembers very few details of this experience, her memory having failed to retain these events.

Only those who have suffered this kind of darkness in their own lives can truly identify with us as I relate these experiences. Why God permits these things to happen, only He knows. We will know by-and-by, but, until then, we only can trust His unfailing love and timing.

Though my brother and his wife say they noticed minute changes in my wife, Peggy, about a week earlier, everything seemed to begin when she spiked a high fever one day. When she mentioned feeling ill, I thought it best to visit the clinic in town. After making an appointment with Peggy's doctor, we drove over to see what help was available.

As is often the case, Peggy was told to take some Tylenol, get some rest, and all should be well. By late afternoon, however, it became obvious Peggy was showing further signs of distress. Once again I called the clinic to tell them Peggy needed additional attention.

When we arrived at the clinic the doctor ordered a series of blood tests. Upon receiving the results of those tests we were told that Peggy would be immediately admitted to the hospital because her white blood cell count was frighteningly low!

My dear wife endured two long weeks in Stephens County Hospital after being diagnosed with pneumonia. Just one week prior to being admitted as a patient, Peggy had retired after working there as a nurse for the previous 20 years. After nursing others for so long, Peggy was now a patient in very serious condition.

Peggy's health seemed to decline with each passing day. Doctors were unable to pinpoint a diagnosis beyond the pneumonia. It was suggested that she had everything from tuberculosis to some kind of leukemia but nobody could find a complete answer to what my wife battled. All I knew for sure was that her health was deteriorating rapidly.

One morning during his rounds, one of the doctors informed me that he did not expect Peggy to survive. He suggested that I call our children and invite them to come to Georgia for one last visit with their mother. In my own devastation I cried to the Lord to have mercy on us and to give us His strength. Our children, Judy from Senegal, West Africa, and Jim from Denver, came as soon as possible to offer support and help in any way possible.

Judy was allotted one month away from her ministry in Africa to come and help. Those first days were spent force-feeding as much Ensure as Peggy could possibly stomach. Unable to tolerate anything else, Ensure, packed with vitamins and minerals, seemed to do the trick in providing sustenance to my dear wife.

Two weeks later, shortly after Peggy had been discharged from the hospital, we sat in the oncologist's office at the Cancer Clinic in Toccoa. Finally, a verdict: Peggy had "the Big C", a rare type of leukemia. Hairy-Cell Leukemia, a cancer of the blood, affects only six to eight hundred people a year in the United States. It is characterized by abnormal changes in white blood cells known as B lymphocytes. The bone marrow creates too many of these defective cells, known as "hairy cells" because of the thin, hair-like projections found on their surface. It occurs more often in men than women and causes susceptibility to infection.

Peggy was to begin treatment the following day at a hospital in Athens, Georgia. My son's wife, Emily, was in town and she, along with Judy, helped make arrangements for getting us to the hospital by 6:30 the next morning. How thankful I was for the help of our children during this time.

This "different kind of darkness," however, began to weigh on me. While the doctor offered some hope of cure, we knew that only God, our Sustainer, was aware of what was to come. The oncologist planned to begin twenty-four hour a day drip treatment of chemotherapy (Cladribine) to last seven straight days. This constant infusion of medical treatment began that very day.

Though the medical team, including nurses and hospital staff, were excellent, Peggy continued to decline, growing weaker and weaker to the point where she could not stand unaided. She was often in terrible pain and even regular injections of morphine did not seem to alleviate her suffering. As I helped feed her and take care of her other personal needs, I tried to be brave and not succumb to my intense emotions.

Throughout the entire seven day ordeal of chemotherapy treatment Judy was with me in Athens helping care for Peggy. During these four weeks of

Peggy's hospitalization, the help of loved ones and friends proved a magnificent boost.

Judy's in-laws, John and Janine Schultz, were especially helpful, doing our laundry, providing meals and visiting. My brother, John, and his wife also provided much encouragement as did many friends of First Alliance Church of Toccoa. Some, including a lady we barely knew from the Alliance Church in Athens, even offered to spend the night with Peggy in the hospital.

Shari Jalovick, after finishing her 12-hour nursing shift at the hospital in Toccoa, would spend all night with Peggy often bringing gifts of homemade, delicious, banana bread. After Peggy was finally released from the hospital, Shari continued to visit countless times throughout the next year providing all kinds of aid and encouragement. David, Shari's husband, probably thought he had lost his wife for a good part of that year!

Other folk blessed us with meals and other assistance during that trial. Later we found out that literally hundreds of people around the world were upholding us in prayer during those long months of illness and recuperation. The Body of Christ in action is a wonderful thing and we were recipients of that abundant Christian love.

While in the hospital fighting for her very life, Peggy contracted an infection called mycobacteria chelonae. This infection still remains in her system at times resulting in sores over some part of her body. Many physicians including infection specialists, internists, and a host of the very best doctors in Athens and Emory Hospital in Atlanta in the field of infectious diseases, have attempted a variety of treatments to combat this infection.

Peggy has endured numerous rounds of antibiotics (some exotic ones), injections, and further hospital stays in her fight against this disease. Some of the worst sores have necessitated lancing under anesthesia because of their size. How thankful we are that, though much money has been spent, God faithfully provided all we have needed.

Trying to discern the light at the end of the tunnel during the two years following her leukemia treatment proved to be difficult. In the darkness, however, the light of Gods' faithfulness has never been extinguished. In spite of all she has been through, Peggy has maintained a joyous heart.

Even today when people ask how she is doing, Peggy answers, "just fine" or "I'm feeling great." Even on days when she does not feel particularly well, after all she has endured, the present is much better than what she has suffered. As for me, after thinking I would lose my beloved wife two years ago, I am just thankful for each extra day we have together.

Having conquered this darkest of valleys, we can only praise our Lord for His innumerable blessings and His unfailing goodness. His light has been shed upon us even in this different darkness. Gladly we give Him all praise and honor for His mercy and grace, for help we received, for friends who went farther than the second mile, and for His incredible faithfulness to two of His children. No matter how black the darkness, or what kind of darkness one faces, His Light can overcome!

Chapter Fifteen

INTO HIS MARVELOUS LIGHT

It is possible that the reader of these stories has never "seen the Light." The Scriptures teach that "Light has come into the world, but people loved darkness instead of light because their deeds were evil" (John 3:19).

In that same gospel, John gives us the words of Jesus who said "I am the light of the world. Whoever follows me will never walk in darkness, but will have the light of life" (John 8:12).

God's desire is that we not only hear and see the light but that we will be those who truly come out of darkness and into His marvelous light (I Peter 2:9). In every nation of this earth are found those who have experienced the transition out of the darkness and into light. It is a marvelous miracle of the grace of God which can be experienced by anyone who believes in Jesus Christ, the One whom God has sent.

One might read the accounts in this book and think to themselves, "Nice story; but it has never happened to me." Well, it *can* happen to you! And only those who have come out of darkness into His marvelous light will dwell with that Light in glory forever.

My desire is that you come to know Jesus Christ, the only Light, and be transformed by His mighty power. This is not a religion, but a personal relationship with the true Light of God. He wants you to be transferred from the kingdom of darkness to the kingdom of light.

As is told in this book, many people living in dark areas of this world such as Tamba, Foday, and Isaac have discovered this Light for themselves and have found that this is where life really begins! You can choose to know the Light just like they have if you so desire! Come **out of darkness** and begin your experience of living in the Light.

Made in the USA
Charleston, SC
25 October 2012